POETRY PROJECT

FOUR

edited by
JOEL RUDINGER

BGSU FIRELANDS LIBRARY

Cambric Press
312 Park Street
Huron, OH 44839

Copyright ©1985, by Cambric Press

All rights reserved. No part of this book may be reproduced in any form without expressed written consent from the publisher. Manufactured in the United States of America.

The poems of Michael Waldecki were previously published in his book *The Electric Volume I* (1983). The poems of Clare Mills were previously published in *The Plough: North Coast Review.*

Cover art by Joel Rudinger

ISBN 0-918342-22-8

Editor's Headnote

The names of many of the contributors may be familiar ones to the readers of Poetry Project Four. Many have regularly appeared in small magazines and presses across the United States and Canada. In addition, a number of the poets here have books in major bookstores which are at this moment carving out reputations.

The voices have never been stronger. Nor have they been as dissimilar in their presentation of the spectrum of experience. The voices of these poets proclaim the strong and cogent individuality that makes poetry so great an art and so fascinating a human force.

CONTENTS

David A. Adams	Great Grandmother Vistula	11
James C. Baloian	what the blind dream of	13
Panos D. Bardis	Cicadas: The Tragic Troubadours	14
Steven Ronald Brattman	Class B Stranded	22
	Islands of Fame	22
Marilyn Salzl Brinkman	I'm One of Them	23
	Woman, You Might As Well Be Dead!	24
Wendy C. Brooks	Busy Signals	25
Judith Cody	Watching Half-Dome from Yosemite Valley	26
	The Woman Who Touched the Sea Male	27
Elaine Dallman	Maria Bonnifemme Died in 1672	33
	Later	34
Laura Dennison	Disco	35
Gwen S. Fick	Hostage	36
	A Visit from Three Clowns	37
John Gery	Being and Tire	38
Arthur Ginsberg	After We Are Gone	40
Catherine Grogan	Gathering In	41
	kitchen poem	42
Richard Hay	Lost a Sympathy Vote	43
	Love Out of Season	44
	Profound	44
Mary Ann B. Henning	Jim	46
Susan A. Katz	The Scent	49
Judy Klare	Company Houses	50
	Summer Living	51
	Old Settlers	52
Aaron Kramer	Phone Calls	53
Jack Lindeman	Sentimentality	57
Mary Peat McDonald	The Listening Heart	58
	Transmigration	59

Raeburn Miller	The Biblical Sense	60
	A Man's Reach	61
	Claim	62
Clare Mills	Tory's Return	63
	Skid Row	64
	My Ax	65
Susan Packie	On Artificial Flowers	66
Thomas Paladino	Out of the Past	68
Michael Joseph Phillips	Five Thematic Variations on Candy	69
	Seen 7/1/83	70
	Kim Alexis	70
	Sybil Danning	70
	Kelli	70
	1983 girls	71
	Doll	71
	Lolita	71
J.F. Pytko	Five Points	72
	Sparrows and Stuffed Owls	73
Odiel Sainte	The Star Diner	75
	Heiligenstadt Lilac	77
M.P.A. Shaeffer	A-B-C's	79
Jon Stefan	Blackbirds	80
John Svehla	Big Bull Cable	82
	A Blown Bird	83
	A Rusty Wind	83
David Swain	Amnesia	84
	Cool Air	84
W. Edgar Vinacke	El Morro	85
	The Silver Forest	86
Michael E. Waldecki	At the Pain of Death	89
	Socially Tyrannosaur	90
Marty Walsh	The Ice Holds Tight	91
	Simon Says	92
	Gretel	94
	The Japanese Print	97

Joan Yarnell	Moonbeam	98
	Shadows of Gray	98
	Gabriel	99
Contributor Notes		100

POETRY PROJECT

FOUR

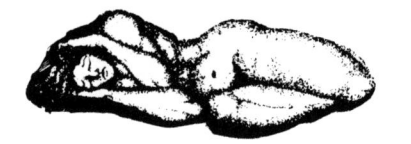

GREAT GRANDMOTHER VISTULA

I write this when my brain is dull,
no inspiration, gray sky, empty
of dreams, no hope. See how little
can be done to curse or cure
the witch of the coldest river.

I am living with the stone mother;
her face turns my bones to water.
Impossible to write under these conditions,
yet I try and fail, deep winter of soul.

Have I experienced everything I can
at forty; am I finished? I can't seem
to find the meaning no matter how hard
I try. Play the Beethoven sonatas again?
Write great poetry? Shall I make
my love with strength? Have great insights
into sin? It all seems to miss the mark.
Will I overcome this frozen flesh,
become a saint at last,
devoted into deep old age?

Something monstrously mundane
seems to be following my footsteps,
the marsh monster of the Polish wiers,
my Great Grandmother of the Vistula.
It was She who spawned my own great-
great grandmother who unraveled
her quilt in a Russian winter,
walked out on the Neva ice and sank
without a sound. I see the wind
scatter little pellets of ice
after her down the freezing hole.

There is no loving memory of her
steely hair, her fingers pricked
with pins of a thousand stitches.
I seem to have to pay the price
of her sacrifice, rising from my
marriage bed on a gray morning,
led by her breath to a cool room
of watching ghosts.

The old woman rocks in a chair
full of icicles; she is knitting me
a scarf, animal hair and broken dreams.
She follows no pattern; it is my life
running beneath her needles, clicking
in the frozen air like her tiny shoes
over the hard surface of the winter
river. Her hand reaches out
of the pool; it beckons me to enter
with a persuasion as long as her
index fingernail.

It is hard to write
with a handful of numbing ancestors
around my blue tugging wrists.
It is hard to turn away
from her tempting smile full of teeth.

David A. Adams

what the blind dream of

there is a difference
of flesh

of how far
to step
after the wind passes

of whose words
you should

listen to next,
and always
the edge
of your own hands...

two stumps
growing eyes
blind as your own

James C. Baloian

CICADAS
THE TRAGIC TROUBADOURS

"Cicadas in a forest that sit upon a tree and pour forth their lily-like voice."
> Homer, *Iliad,* III, 151-152

"The chirping cicada sits on a tree and pours down his shrill song continually from under his wings in the season of wearisome heat."
> Hesiod, *Works and Days,* 682-684

"The Athenians were among the first to lay aside their arms and, adopting an easier mode of life, to change to more luxurious ways. And the elderly men of the wealthier class gave up...fastening their hair in a knot with a golden cicada."
> Thucydides, *Histories,* I, vi, 3

"To fast and sing like a cicada."
> Aristophanes, *The Clouds,* 1360

Cicadas, "the prophets of the Muses who sing above our heads."
> Plato, *Phaedrus,* 262d

"The singing cicadas are males, the others are females."
> Aristotle, *Historia Animalium,* 556b

"She's naught but skin and bones. Pray, does she feed on dewdrops like a cicada?"
> Theocritus, *Shepherds,* 15-16

"*Cicada cicadae cara, formicae formica*" ("Cicada is dear to cicada, ant to ant").
> Latin proverb

"*Sole sub ardenti resonant arbusta cicadis*" ("The copses under the burning sun ring with the shrill cicada's voice").
> Vergil, *Eclogae,* II, 13

"Et cantu querulae rumpent arbusta cicadae" ("And the plaintive cicadas rend the thickets with song").
                       Vergil, *Georgicon,* III, 328

"Vere prius volucres taceant, aestate cicadae" ("Sooner would birds be silent in spring, or cicadas in summer").
                       Ovid, *Artis Amatoriae,* I, 271

"They used to eat even cicadas and grasshoppers as an incentive to appetite."
                       Athenaeus, *Deipnosophists,* 133b

I. Resurrection

Digging, climbing, crawling, creeping,
Never napping, never sleeping,
Nymph and empress from the deep!
Pluto's Kingdom,
Years of darkness,
The grim shadows,
All have lost their reins and chains.
Ah, the riddle and arcanum:
Broken skins and shattered tombs;
Then, the light of Resurrection!

II. Life in a Cemetery

Creamy-white rise all the nymphs.
And the shrubs, the trees, the woodlands
Now become a vast graveyard:
Clinging skins on twigs and branches,
Empty shells and twisted frames,
Golden-brown crypts, coffins, caskets,
Sepulchers, and cenotaphs.
And the glassy wings flash omens,

Veins that curve and form dark signs,
Wars forecasting
Everlasting,
Trumpets blasting,
Sabers clashing,
Fury, frenzy, blood, and death.

III. Ephemeral Feast

Summer waning.
Death is gaining.
Melancholy, sad cicadas,
Feast on sap, the sweetest nectar,
Feast on sap and make a rain.
Flocks of birds! Cicada-killers
Seek your flesh to feed their babes.
Make a rainbow.
Make a sundog,
Spectral sundog.
Make an iris—
Flaming, flaring,
Shining, sparkling,
Brilliant iris—
Make a rainbow
And an iris
To confuse your hungry foes.

IV. The Last Lament

Loudest insect,
Tragic singer,
Transient star of melody,
Tune your chambers,
Tune your tymbals,
Magic cymbals,

Drums, and timbrels.
Sing a song.
Cronus-bitten,
With heart smitten,
Sing a dirge by Clotho written.
Sing a dirge with drums vibrating,
Resonating,
Stridulating,
Sing your intermittent song—
Flowing, piercing,
Buzzing, hissing,
Humming, whistling—
Sound your box from dawn to dusk.
Call your mate with flute-shrill rhythms
And your mandolin-soft tunes,
Call your mate for time is fleeting.
And before you meet with Charon,
Fly to Eunomis the harpist
To consume Aristo's pride:
Touch the harp, the broken string,
And with Eunomis now sing—
Drums vibrating,
Resonating,
And with sorrow stridulating!

V. Kyoto Festival

Bring rice paper,
Ringed bamboos, and make a kite.
Make a hundred,
Make a thousand,
Fill the sky.
Make cicada-kites and paint them,
Paint them dark with shades foreboding,
Paint them bright with hues exploding.
Fill the wings.

Fill the wings with trees and flowers,
Castles, towers,
Hailstorms, showers.
Fill the wings with beasts and creatures—
Horses neighing,
Serpents swaying,
Demons dancing,
Dragons prancing.
Fill the wings with plants and beasts.
Listen! Listen!
The New Year!
Listen! Listen!
Death is near!
For your birth means death tonight
In the waltzing of the kite.
Listen! Listen!
Life is death and death is life
In the realm of endless strife.
Listen! Listen!
Hate is love and love is hate
In the wheel of cruel Fate.
Ah, the stars! The torrid Taurus,
Aries, Cetus,
Pisces, Lepus,
Bright Orion, and Centaurus,
High above the wailing chorus—
Drums vibrating,
Drums pulsating,
Stridulating,
Ululating
For the vanities of life.

VI. Cathay's Chu-ki

Princes bringing jade cicadas
For the princes that have slept,
And the soldier heals his wounds
With the *chu-ki*—
Scarlet salve and bright-red balsam.
My beloved!
By your tomb,
Joyless, sobbing, and heartbroken,
Now I count the jade cicadas
That adorn your sacred gates
And your temple's every portal—
Magic windows
Chaining demons
In the chambers of black Hell.
Yang the jade and Yin all evil,
Galaxies of amulets,
Coruscating constellations,
Astral streams, sublime formations,
And your philomelic tongue
All bespangled with the brightest
Gem of all.
Ah, my cage, my dismal prison!
Ah, my mournful, plaintive song!
Life is death without your kisses
And the music of your voice.
But my dirge, cicada-dirge,
Life will give to the two starlets—
Sapphire windows of your soul.
And our *ch'an*, unbroken chain—
Yesterday-today-tomorrow—
Will unite, with golden links,
Our two dazzling, floral kingdoms,
Our two beaming, gleaming worlds!

VII. Siamese Hunt

New cicada-killers hunting!
Mountain-mapping,
Never napping,
Wildly yapping,
Insect-trapping.
Hungry butchers go night-hunting!
Firewood snapping,
They are tapping,
Rudely rapping,
Fiercely slapping,
Madly clapping.
Now the ladies, swarms of ladies,
Seek their lovers.
Ah, the blazing, brilliant flames!
Conflagration
And cremation!
Love is death and death is life
Round forbidding Nastrand's knife.

VIII. The Trojan Prince

Handsome prince, fair Eos' lover,
How celestial is your bond!
Golden summers, life eternal,
Rapture, bliss, enchantment, joy,
Ecstasy, angelic madness,
Burning passion, thrilling union,
Fiery furor, frenzy, rage!
Blind Tithonus!
Race on Time's unending orb.
Shiver,
Quiver,
Quake and shake.
Choose the rose without its thorns.

Shrivel, shrink and sink and shudder,
Wither, waste and wane and ebb.
Take the year without a winter.
Tremble, dwindle, crumble, cringe.
Take the day, forget the night.
Flinch and fade and fall and falter.
Vanish!
Ah, the horror,
Damnedest horror,
Deadly horror!
Vanish! Vanish!
Life eternal,
Hell supernal,
Damnedest bliss!
Weep, Tithonus!
Wail, Tithonus!
Howl, Tithonus!
Clasp the moon without its halo,
Take a fair but silent Freya,
Snatch a bloom with wilting petals,
Catch a tongueless nightingale,
While the stars are still gyrating,
Fulgurating,
Radiating,
Coruscating,
Scintillating;
For the cosmic end is near!
Curse, Tithonus!
Shriek and shrill and screak and screech—
Drums vibrating,
Drums pulsating,
Resonating,
Stridulating,
Ululating!

      Panos D. Bardis

CLASS B STRANDED

Trees surrounding.
Teacher dead.
Food gone.
Injuries.

Sky red
At the beach.
Only tide pools
Alive.

Gleaming white
Missile
With fire behind
A second before.

                  Steven Ronald Brattman

ISLANDS OF FAME

Islands of fame
Orange in the green sea.

                  Steven Ronald Brattman

I'M ONE OF THEM

Hard and weathered
   like old bones

A concert of gray granite,
   feldspar, shale, slate
      and glittering mica

A cemetery of color
   like broken crayons in boxes

Freezing and thawing
   shifting like a chest

Rising and falling
   shaving little fragments off

I start to turn to dust.

                    Marilyn Salzl Brinkman

WOMAN, YOU MIGHT AS WELL BE DEAD.

Woman, you might as well be dead
your skin is like old wood
weathered and dry
with wavy strips of gray
streaking your hands and arms
like rings in trees
your senses swing
like fern fronds in moist air
drugged with the scent of pain
blood bone and flesh
what good are they
when cancer has eaten away the mind

                                        Marilyn Salzl Brinkman

BUSY SIGNALS

The leering telephone smirks from its corner
While the stereo sings Love Songs,
And I play chess with myself.
The last time I saw him
Comes again like a murdering stage of phantoms
Leering like the telephone
And the words beat my temples
With brutal laughter.

Smirking in its corner,
Laughing at me,
Me
Cut off and guessing.
Blindly alone,
Alone in cold deathly dark
With all the rules changed.

Wendy C. Brooks

WATCHING HALF-DOME FROM YOSEMITE VALLEY

Supine, through the cradle of my thighs
I watch the sun slowly set between my legs.
It descends beneath the birth bone
disappears and forms a flaming halo through my pubic hair.

Curls are solar flares seen through the red mist.

This is my day, I have taken its last display
into a dark place where I embrace it,
grasp it firmly by its flaming tail
and watch it sprawl against the grass
beside me.

Prone, over the ledge of my arms
I watch the stars rise outside my head,
they ascend over thought
and point white slivers at my naked back.

Cold shouts through the dark.

I am beyond cold sounds,
no white sliver will frighten me.
I have wrestled with the day
and here between my body and the ground
I press the heated red distress
like grapes.

The sun has gone into the moon cave
I lock the entrance
with a small twist of my ankles.

In the black night the day is mine
where I can probe the waning warmth
with my own flame,

and study the shape of noon,
recall the sun rise over a half-dome
and wrap around the afternoon
a crescent prison with my ribs.

      Judith Cody

THE WOMAN WHO TOUCHED THE SEA MALE

It is Monterey Bay
stuck out
curled around the edge
of the Pacific Ocean.

Air clear as diamond
cold, windless,
becalms me.

I burrow into the warm sand.

A crab or shrike
will surely pass me by.

The foam passes over my ankles.

Birds call to one another,
sand grass bends.

The surf passes over my knees.

Steady thrills of great water
pound through my skin.

Only a Pacific wind
can be as sudden,
there is no time
to cover eyes,
sand blasts into hair
skin folds, tongue
is grit covered,
my sand crater is flooded
by a cold sucking pool.

Afterquiet.

He gurgles and gasps
clutches his throat
all the while he stares at me
through lashless, golden eyes.

A wet, tangled heap,
he sprawls where the wave
has washed him ashore
close beside me on the sand,
wads of kelp wind through his legs.

Sea Male
cripple by water weeds
helpless, heaved up on the beach.

I had never dreamed
the Sea Male's skin
would gleam
like a deep copper mirror
(his thighs are warm fleshed).

I had never dreamed
that I would be lying
face to startled face

(his ears are merely soft dimples)
with this alien male.

The surf passes over my mouth.

(And his mouth).

I choke
yet he relaxes
inhales the salty water
inhales it deeply
with gentle satisfaction.

Sunlight shimmers over the copper skin
like on a moving mirrored surface
as he picks away the soggy weeds
then arranges himself
(as polite as a Prime Minister)
not even kelp covers him now.

Wind begins to hum
over the wide bay, over Monterey
over Santa Cruz,
over my ear tips.

The surf laps against my belly.

Sea Male smiles,
slowly dips his head into water
for every breath
(his breathing is meditation—like the whale's).

From his navel to his groin
the deep vertical Treasure Slit
is sealed.

"Reach in," he beckons to me

"Reach in..." his fingers force his belly wide apart,
"Your hand will fit—
it is designed for this—
Reach in...probe...take what you feel."

Air is wet and windy,
surly water
growls against us.

The water thuds against my back.

"Yes...yes,"
like the wind
he hums "yes...yes...I am come
from another side of today."

Like the wind
his words sting my ears,
"yes...I am come from yesterday."

Like the surf
his words pulse,
"yes...yes...yesterday...
yes...yes...tomorrow...
yes...reach in...feel the future...
yes...yes...reach in me...in me...in me."

I reach,
touch flesh
and I falter.

"Yes...in me...touch future."

The ocean swells to my chin.

Like the shell,
his warm chamber

twists and curves
where I explore,
feel his prize,
palm slips beneath it,
sinews tighten,
fingers curl,
wrapped around
his one possession
my hand emerges
in my air.

"No...I've never seen it...no."

The tide sucks at my toes.

Sun is splintered on the water
moon holds back the waves
Sea Male stares in horror,
his ocean moves away,

Like the tide
his voice
is ebbing,
"no...no...today...today."

Like the moon
his voice
is pale,
"no...give me...come to the sea...
come to the sea...no...no...give it to me...
no...no...come with me."

Can I reach inside again?
No. No. He is dull and parched
his belly sealed forever
forever.

The ocean slaps the sand far away.

Sea Male
crawls along the sand,
reaches water,
turns,
cries,
"O...give it back...come with me."

The Pacific arcs and takes him.

Yes. I will. I will.

The ocean heaves like hatred.

Like the gull's
my voice
is little
in this place.

                                       Judith Cody

MARIA BONNIFEMME DIED IN 1672

Her aunt used to say Maria glided her tongue
across stone walls.
She needed coolness. She was five.

Moving behind their gauze screen, she turns
within the cloistering family;
she (or someone) poisons that aunt, two uncles,
a younger brother.

An adolescent, she visits the hospital;
the softness of small firm breasts,
her saint-like thinness, are noted.
Four patients die.

The black frocked men of the town
know Maria is the betrayer:
"Burn out the roots
which terrify women and men."
They sign this statement.

Then they watch the movement
to the right, to the left, of fire.
Trance-watching is burning her to nakedness.
They watch the fire's
play with the blistering skin.

In 1676, protecting themselves with toads, people
dig in the wheat fields away from the town
to find her bones.

She has given proof: the poisonings continue.

They take charred bones,
place the relics before faces of plaster
in front of the altars.
They genuflect. They ignite incense.

Elaine Dallman

LATER

High bare white walls
and the fact of separation.
We talk of ex-spouses.
We believed marriage
shook bells of incense.

We talk.
My cousin told me you had stared
down the aisle.
You clasped the rail
so it would be bruised,
if a wrist.

I return your faded blanket,
your dried auto-glove,
your blue beret from Basque country.

You're a traveler with tales of escape,
your eyes, harder—
the way the film of incandescent porch light
mingles with city air.

Elaine Dallman

DISCO

Into space they stare
and, moving lips, mouth air.

They listen to disco and they twist,
let bodies go in empty tryst,

go nowhere. They want vacancy.
They'd rather not exist than be.

But sinking deeply into sound,
they go, they go, they go around.

They do not talk, their bodies do.
They are not interested in you.

Their bodies move in towers of fire
and ice, of cold and hot desire.

But scared to build, terrified to mate,
they sizzle down, they separate.

They only clown, they don't create...
go nowhere, turn, evaporate....

Laura Dennison

HOSTAGE

Not afraid to die,
Yet not desirous of it,
One accepts the possibility
When one accepts the diplomat's
Wire-walking trade.
As the summer laborer complains
That it's humidity, not heat,
That enervates,
So it is not death, but insecurity,
That weighs.
Hours of ennui,
And idle days
Follow like artificial pearls
On a string,
Worthless each,
Except as a priceless day
In its owner's life,
Overtly wasted.

One wonders what is being gained,
What holocaust held off,
What games of international nerves
Brought to a harmless end.
The answers hang delayed.
One turns involuntarily to old, old anchorage—
Hope,
Love of homeland,
Duty tended,
And desperate blind faith.

Gwen S. Fick

A VISIT FROM THREE CLOWNS

The first clown peeped through the door
With a bulbous nose
And a grin all over his face.
He quacked at me like a duck,
But I didn't laugh.
There's enough to laugh at in life
Without that parody!

The second clown wore too-big feet
And a red-haired, stand-up wig.
He waggled his tongue at me,
But I wasn't amused.
I picked up my son's toy rattle
And flung it at him.
There's enough of amusement in life
Without that absurdity!

A court jester hopped in the window,
Small, wizened,
Wearing a three-pointed camp a-jingle with bells.
He smacked my knee
With a silly, inflated bladder.
I called him a nasty name.
He jiggled a jig,
Bounced to the windowsill,
Turned and pointed a single, impudent thumb.
"Thou hadst better laugh," he declaimed,
"Or else thou'lt surely weep!"
And I did weep,
For what he had said
Wasn't funny!

                              Gwen S. Fick

BEING AND TIRE

> Dasein is always ambiguously "there"— that is to say, in that public disclosedness of Being-with-one-another where the loudest idle talk and the most ingenious curiosity keep "Things moving," where, in an everyday manner, everything (and at bottom nothing) is happening.
> —Heidegger

How will they remember me,
these boys with their baseball bat
watching me across the street
change my tire? That little fat

one in red stripes, his round mouth
open wide, is so precisely
vacant I could be TV
or a northern snowstorm nicely

rolled into a snowman, for
all his peanut eyes can tell
at this distance, just too far
for him or his pals to yell

over to. I raise my hand
but I'm not of their kind, spirits
from some curious netherland,
one which draws me here to hear its

echoes: the gangly, overgrown
punk in tattered dungarees
talking wildly, his clone
bent and picking from his knees

scabs concealed beneath fresh dirt,
and the midget wearing glasses
too big for him—nothing, at
bottom nothing moving, passes

these boys by, not me, nor snow,
nor what matters in this world.
My tire changed, they'll let me go
back to my existence, hurled.

                              John Gery

AFTER WE ARE GONE

Looking back from under this green field
is easy. I choose a morning in spring
when her prickly breath tickles our stems.
Daughters' soft steps can be felt from afar,
as they approach we nod and bow gallantly,
not unlike the rocking that went on
in old age. Today we hold hands
as they peer into blue centers.
Their love descends our stems
deep to placid hearts. Once
we stood near this place to watch
another daughter bedded in oiled wood
slip on silent pulleys into the earth.
One comes to know the roll and bump
of this ground, the sprinkling from
so many eyes nourishing our place.
Miriam is sniffing just like she did
in the dahlias years ago, I can feel
her fingers on the cup of my flower
and yours. When they leave
you and I will rest awhile, our petals
                          breathless in the wind

                    Arthur Ginsberg

GATHERING IN

The fruit's in flower.
Vines twist over the trellis, lace like.

Apples, near to bursting, skin red and tight.
So many of them!
Produced as thoughtlessly as children.

Pears sit in silence.
Their fat green bottoms rest
in the palm of my hand.

Piled high in the woven baskets,
the fruits are still,
heavy and quiet.

Resting in the bright sunlight
they connect, mouths open,
ripening and bleeding.

       Catherine Grogan

kitchen poem

fragrant smells
light on the table

thick soup steam rising
the bowls the spoons

hot liquid spilling down a chin
warm egg noodles slipping out of slight

vegetables from the garden—
bits of tomato, beans and corn

bubbling and boiling
overflowing the pot

                              Catherine Grogan

LOST A SYMPATHY VOTE FOR LOVE

Suicide was the last thing in
  the world he would ever serious-
  ly contemplate
Still he swam further and further
  from the shore

After every few strokes of his
  arms he would glance back at
  her lying on the blanket
No she did not look his way and
  no she did not jump up call
  and wave frantically for him
  to return

This scheme of his failed and
  it had lasted at least half
  an hour
Before entering the water he held
  her in an embrace and asked if
  she loved him. She wasn't sure
  as there was a boy back home
  who she also cared for deeply
No she couldn't say which would be
  the one to gain all her love

Richard F. Hay

LOVE OUT OF SEASON

Artie Shaw played a part—
He set the mood with his record
   "Begin the Beguine."
That was the song played
often at Bulloughs Pond
Back in the winter of '42.

The boys watched the girl
Skate from afar
And thought how wonderful
It would be to skate together.
I think his friend spoiled it for him
When he asked her,
"Wouldn't you like to skate with Joe?"
"No, I wouldn't," she replied.

Joe got over it in time
But every so often
He hears "Begin the Beguine"
And thinks not of tropical islands
But rather of Bulloughs Pond
In winter.

                              Richard F. Hay

PROFOUND

It was more of a lecture
   than a conversation

It took place several years ago
   while we were on vacation

   My memory fades to the extent
   that even the subject matter
   is lost

What I will always remember is
   how logical and profound
I thought my statements to be

That is, until I saw the tear
   rolling down my daughter's cheek

                      Richard F. Hay

JIM

As I stood cleaning
Those horrid green beans
More rotten
Than good

My thoughts
Of you
Turned
My mind

To the inevitable
Day
Of
Parting

Saying
"ALL
GOOD THINGS
END"

So
why
Cry
Tears?

That's
Life's
Final
Angel

Of harshness.
LIFE,
Destiny's
Echo.

In my
Brain's
Attic

Thoughts
Memories
Of smiles
Crystallized

On the
Canvas and
Life's
Sharing

With you
Caring
Laughing
Missing

Life
With
Your
Style

Is
Vacant
Void
Of

You
You
Always
You

Of
Whom
Are
Painted

Traces
Of
Your
Voice

In my
Mind's
Eye
Lid

Embracing
What
Can not
Be
Said.

                              Mary Ann B. Henning

THE SCENT

    You sleep
like something that has died
hiding the animal-light behind
closed lids the small
sigh of your breathing calls
me to you.

    I come
nocturnally to prowl
to stiffen at your scent
you neither threaten
nor respond but lie
baited beneath what passes
for desire in my eyes.

    Something old
in me remembers clinging
nakedly to trees and aches
to hone itself against
your flesh my breath comes hot
and hard and it would
burn you if it could.

    Your scent
is strong and silently commanding
tamely I am inching up the limp
length of you your body ripening
in sleep your dreams kindling
to my flame purring
I come rubbing my lips against
the primal pleasure
of your frame.

                              Susan A. Katz

COMPANY HOUSES
(Haydenville, Ohio in 1954)

Their bare yards
wear a kind of beauty in reverse,
each house repeating the same spare slogans.

One crazy-eyed outhouse
relieves the serial symmetry,
one blessed gate has opened, out of line.

The scene passes, like a filmstrip of days,
Sunday that one red blanket
hanging on the coal-grey week.

                                    Judy Klare

SUMMER LIVING
(As depicted in the New York *Times* Magazine section.)

Summer Living lives in white Mediterranean rooms,
perfect flowers look in at all the doors,
shine in all its mirrors. It wears white;
it drinks rakish things
from marvelous vacuum-bound cups
and eats from plates
in living Picasso.

My summer life sweats, gets dirty, swears;
my flowers, displaced, need care. My woods need paint.
My whites despair.
But my nights are raisin colored, just as those,
my dawn is chartreuse too;
abandoning various winters,
all of us idolize the same bright light.

Judy Klare

OLD SETTLERS

Brandywine Drive, Mid Road. These names suggest
battles with both man and nature,
each anecdote a silent bequest.

They thought they reasonsed they were meant to be here.
They left names like Conscience Pier,
Sinai, Jericho, Mt. Misery Point;
they borrowed Poquott, Happauge, Syosset,
filling in the rest with practical notions—
Wading River, Bread and Cheese Road,
Baiting Hollow Turnpike, Quaker Path.

They knew what they were doing all along.
No hang-ups with ecology, or God's wrath,
no Indian trouble, no sense of wrong.

         Judy Klare

PHONE CALLS

I.

Poor Jean, with never a trick or a joke!
Lips locked, you have managed it after all.
Imagine me craving now the rebuke
of your hourlong bi-monthly call!

II.

Since she's already ten years older
than I was at my father's death,
and has already explained to her child
a grandmother's death,
and when it was her turn to ask I told her candidly,
why do I feel now, finger just raised from the dial,
guilty of something, some error of omission,
of having perhaps not often enough repeated
that every boon has to be paid for,
including the blue of her eyes
by which Ben, whose burial takes place on Tuesday,
was astounded the day they opened.

III.

And so the phone call ended; there was time
for others on the list, but they could wait.
Coffee as well would have involved the crime
of opening one's mouth; best face the gate,
and when *it* opened, trudge inside the train
and through a sooty window watch the sky's
appropriate grayness drop appropriate rain
to reprimand the dryness of one's eyes.
This left an hour and a half or more
out of whose hush a requiem might be wrung

before one reached his depot, then his door,
with a bizarre contagion on the tongue.

IV.

The call came months past my urge to send him a card
with only a question mark on it; he uttered the word
easily now (if the first time, to her, it fell hard)
and strangely his story was not the most startling I'd heard:
how soon he'd persuaded her it was all for the best
(though she'd struggled awhile and maintained she could make
  things last)
and how calm their theatrical daughter was, having guessed
at his new stage, new dialogue, new cast.

But somehow, although I was not struck dumb at his news,
once the call ended I felt a compulsion to close
the book I'd been putting my brain to, and sat stunned
as if unable to bounce back from a bruise,
as if those syllables were a series of blows,
as if I'd been asked to absorb the death of a friend.

V.

Two weeks have passed since the first call came;
how then can it be to blame?
Nor did it come from him to me,
but from wife to wife in secrecy:
No longer would he go to his job,
nor Fridays to his district club,
nor to the window for sun or moon,
nor open a paper, nor lift a spoon,
nor, when she spoke, admit he heard,
nor open his mouth to let out a word.

Ten days have passed since the worst call came;
how then can it be to blame?
Besides, no germs had been involved;
they'd had a problem—now it was solved.
It wasn't a case of conventional ills,
but merely a matter of seventeen pills.
Besides, it had nothing to do with me:
our date was for seven; he did it at three.

The box was closed by the time we came;
how then can it be to blame?
I did shake hands with each of his sons,
did kiss his wife and his daughter once;
I did look into their eyes, I did—
eyes that, before the glossy lid,
was lowered, had looked their longest and last,
and into mine their look was passed.

A week ago last night we came
back from the wake. Is that to blame?
Is that why my thoughts are astir with *contagion,
symptoms, period of incubation*?

Early this morning I became
aware of something, something to blame.
It's not that I'm medically ill,
but merely a matter of lacking the will
to look at the window or even the wall,
to march my body the length of the hall,
to hear my wife, to lift my head,
to open my mouth for a bite of bread.

VI.

*The time has been my senses would have cooled
to hear* such tidings like a hiss uncoiled—
my gasp would have struck back whoever called:
chill as a tomb.

Now, smoothly, with a secretarial skill,
raising my voice not one note on the scale,
I welcome to the factbox in my skull
the place, the time.

Aaron Kramer

SENTIMENTALITY

If I call you mother
it immediately strikes me
that I have succumbed to sentimentality,
and that is a word I keep trying to avoid.
Our feelings must be hard,
something more akin to our bones
than the gray matter of our brains.
Let me say you called on the phone
and your voice sounded like a popular song
in praise of my nephews.
Your adulation raised thoughts of sentimentality
and I hardened my response
with a stony guffaw.
Yet when you added
in a postscript
that you fell down a flight of rain slick steps
on West Avenue
skinning one of your shins
I scuttled my ramparts
against your old fashioned noun,
for you are eighty
and when the doctors in the hospital
couldn't believe you were more than sixty-five
I too rejoiced,
captivated by a vision
of smooth skin
and the unlabored reality
of your sculptured hairdo.

                        Jack Lindeman

THE LISTENING HEART

Dare one conjecture from the way
A man talks to his child
How he would love with words?
Would the small commands and old endearments
Then, too, cause certain edges of the body
To swell into rosy stones?
Would the inflection of meant for only you
Because you do and do not understand
Still be there also?
Would the wounding softness
Of the murmured breath
Be more or less of either?
And would the imperious impact of the
Tongue's less near caress
Then cause jealousy in sister
Breast and sister thigh?

I should like once to listen to him
Talk to a cold hungry dog.

                                      Mary Peat McDonald

TRANSMIGRATION

What makes it seem to me we two are certain halves
Of something not yet all remembered?
When have I bathed in pools which are your eyes
So that I am to you as I to me?
Why should it be as though your reminiscent palm
Is curved to fit my breast in recollected gentleness
And stir the patient embers of familiar fire?
Why does your voice restore my ear
With dearest sounds I've heard you breathe before—
Before we met?
Shall it be long before the moiety of my lips
Will taste wholeness and perfection
And blood will claim its carmine pulse to praise
Entireness once more?

Mary Peat McDonald

THE BIBLICAL SENSE
> "Not to know mee argues your selves unknown."

At the doorway of the ear
a toad sits.

I think I know.
But truth is like gunpowder,

like smut that lights the sky.
To know oneself

is to be unknown.
To know the angels,

the dark angels, the outstretched
wings, to know

God by his dark likeness—
that is knowledge indeed,

a tree, a sword.

Raeburn Miller

A MAN'S REACH

Memory of touch
is make believe.
All memory shades,

blusters, cajoles.
Of love, one lover,
a love for two hours,

of hands, two hours
of the love of hands,
remembering that.

Well, we
lie a lot.
I have soft hands.

And memory of
touch, and memory
of touch, and

I would want it
not to be that.

Raeburn Miller

CLAIM

How false the sluice stands
when the vein has thinned.

The shallow roots of a cactus
return to mastery,
undisturbed, unaware,
its values more fragile,
more lasting.

The sun is gold.
The sand is gold.

Shadows darken like blood.

The mining timbers slowly skew,
skeletal, the dust pushes.

No one looked forward.
It was as if the mountain
had been built to last.

                               Raeburn Miller

TORY'S RETURN

She had the rough hewn features
    lines of a drunken plowman
high cheekbones
    of a forgotten tribe
Haunting eyes of pain
    slim and flat
    ample bottom
no makeup   world worn
    windblown
        brown pony tie
jeans, blouse and flats
    40's I'd guess
and the softest saddest hands
"It seems like I should know you,"
    she said
"Maybe you do, deja vu—
    in some bar"
    Indelibly burned
    in my mind
The tell-tale story
    in Tory's eyes.

                      Clare Mills

SKID ROW

The guy
With the sallow mouth
Hollowed out eyes
Shakin' bad
Rollin' his own
Lips move constantly
One smoke after another
Pickin' up and stashin'
The bar backy—
    We all got an economy move
    Area's clean
Another smoke

Reminds me of Hobo Jack
Tellin' me
About the guy
Down by the river
Wrapped in the latest news
Mornin' comes
Awake at dawn
Before the clean-up
Or the fuzz
Folds old yesterday's papers
Drops them in the can

Another pint
Another smoke
A new day dawns—

                        Clare Mills

MY AX

The guitar man
Been over many a mile
Three decades and more
With that very special ax
Bonded—and then some
To the end

Never missed a gig
Or let each other down
Really smokin' and those crowds smokin' too
When he lays on those licks
Words & music makin' love
Says just what he feels
On that six string AC job

Not for sale or trade
Time to go
Where the good ones go
Givin' that old black ax
The final supreme tribute
Guitar Hall of Fame
"Hear that plaintive moan?"
Guitar Man

        and HIS AX

                Clare Mills

ON ARTIFICIAL FLOWERS

The room is empty full
With voices rebounding
From wall to wall
Faces smiling
Lips kissing
I hold out my gloved hand
Exchange banalities
You're looking good
It's been so long
We'll have to get together
My eyes can't look ahead
My feet are rooted
To the back of the room
So empty full
Don't they know
She is dead
Don't look at her
It isn't right
That she should be
So exposed
With flowers saying
We can see you
But you can't see us
Evermore
So quiet
With only the pounding
Of silent fists
Against the walls
Of my mind
Only the broken sobs

The canopy is up
Over the grave
We come to visit

Not to stay
They're leaving
The lawn is empty full
Of voices laughing
You too will come this way
I leave with them
And stay behind
The world is empty full

                        Susan Packie

OUT OF THE PAST

Because of impatience,
we are in exile.
Because of impatience,
a bold secular tongue,
we are not ourselves.

That is what he said to me
in the slow falling dusk,
the cold but not clear night.

We had been friends years back
when the faintest stars
in the blackest sky
were omens, when no clues
were in the labors of gratitude.

So I said, crisply I thought,
"To walk alone at night
without a soul in the emptiness
is but to never come home."

We turned then to our business
in the patiently falling dark,
tangled in ambiguity,
and yet still reaching for more.

       Thomas Paladino

FIVE THEMATIC VARIATIONS ON CANDY

1

Colossal titted
Beut bodded Nefertiti—
Bebop sex empres !

2

Go world class show girl,
Sultry hip beauty d' l' Oak,
Top Chicago queen !

3

Sweet street genius,
43rd & Broad's empress curleycue,
48 EE titted thin colossus !

4

Sultry street angel,
Lincoln Blvd. sex flash,
Beut Aphrodite !

5

Cinema sex doll,
Marina Del Rey angel,
Luminescent day empress !

                                        Michael Joseph Phillips

SEEN 7/1/83

Track short genius,
Bluewhitescimpclad tanned empress,
Bloomington goddess !

                                            Michael Joseph Phillips

KIM ALEXIS

Golden Girl divine,
Swing model princess d'83,
Florida phenom !

                                            Michael Joseph Phillips

SYBIL DANNING

Beut-bilt beach empress,
Stacked go hot box fantasy,
Bikini top sensation !

                                            Michael Joseph Phillips

KELLI

I know, i know
I know, i know, i know,
I know, i know !

                                            Michael Joseph Phillips

1983 GIRLS

Times Square paragons,
Hollywood Boulevard flashes,
u.S.A. luv geniuses !

                        Michael Joseph Phillips

DOLL

Sweetpunkclad Venus,
Top action create d' hot summer,
U.S.A. go paragon,
Beut wonder hop girl,
Swingsensation d' '83 !

                        Michael Joseph Phillips

LOLITA

Sweet Venus nymphette,
36" x 24" x 37" 16 yr. old beut,
Me gusto mucho !

                        Michael Joseph Phillips

FIVE POINTS

On the street,
there are no windows
to accentuate the sun.
Steps are imaginary as doors
to stout houses.
Light is a wound,
darkness a developing scar.

I walk from end
to endless end
and try to recall children,
singing with the sky's voices.
But what I remember
is how birds were pinned
to the nails in capstoned walls,
and how their wings
were like ferns clutched by frost—
dead, brown...
in less than a day.

In the wind,
stiff as a bone,
there is a sound:
like someone choking.

J.F. Pytko

SPARROWS AND STUFFED OWLS

After a fortnight of Spring,
there was no question about
the winter and where it was.
A world of footprints criss-crossed
the unmapped snow.
Everyone moved like Eskimos
in cramped igloos.
No one said hello.

The branches of sycamores
were imprisoned in ice.
At yellow sunsets,
they looked like a maze
of lights strung by a spider.
Fuel was low.
We were enjoined to conserve it
by those who didn't.
What could they do to us
if we didn't care to freeze to death?
They needed our votes
to keep warm,
to self-create auras with the breaths
as they promised to keep
the unkept promises before a trip
to the Caribbean where promises
are sandcastles completed a moment
prior to a rising tide.

The children built snowmen.
Into eye holes they put round
little notes that said— coal eyes.
Broomsticks were unavailable,
and sold for fuel.

We made no promises
about next year's supply
and helped them build bigger snowmen
to develop a constituency
of a laugh.
The children didn't care
about when winter would end
and reminded us that Spring
is a state of mind.

                              J.F. Pytko

THE STAR DINER

        Where the
mirrors met at the corner
diner,
        a waitress appearing in
three perspectives
                rose on one
table, pink in a glass all
over the room.

        You had
just reached in to unfold it, all
arms dipping,
            whether the dust which on
one side seemed was
                not in the center—
the coffee cup—worn
lacquer exposing a

presence, truly cement lapped
up at you;
        focused on one salt
cellar
        cut like a diamond, no
doubt, whose image if seen from the
ceiling, bounced through

jungles of rubberplant. You, you had
hardly considered
            how these might
multiply uninhibited
—more than by
            just three dimensions

—the flashing sign by a road, and good food at a reasonable price.

                                        Odiel Sainte

HEILIGENSTADT LILAC

It was
harder to tell
than breeze from wind

and grew much darker.

Scattering on
Beethovengang or
wherever

this might have been,

blossoms had gathered
small storms
where they were

brushed along pavements.

Harder to tell than
reeds from tall grass—
strange

differences.

As flush across tiger
lily from lily,
that much more strange in its

markings, a dappled
illiterate script

This one seam from which
one drawstring ran back
unravelling everything

thin as air is to
ozone it hung
spinning that ray on the same

prismatic
edge without shape.

This was
it though, it seemed
caught in its most

transparent version.

A switch broken off
it fell
bright dreamthread in dark

colors of lilac,

and ran by the brook
farther down until

stung by its own
force into waking, it
grew, gathered, stuck

on some

shameless, colloquial place.

Odiel Sainte

A-B-C'S

What face have I seen
In the misty looking-glass of years?
What form struggles through
The wrinkles of cobwebs,
Through the thin parchment of dust?

Is it the searching face
Of a grown man, in that glass
Looking over his shoulder,
Searching for his childhood
Like a broken plaything in the toybox,

Seeking to discover himself
Again among the butterfly wings
Of his toy soldier days
Somewhere in the corner
Of memory's nursery?

M.P.A. Shaeffer

BLACKBIRDS

peeling oranges in the morning
a copper potato knife
the skins piled in her dresser drawer
lemon grapefruit half eaten peanutbutter jars
sounds of a gramophone
from the bible stand, raked
like a dying man after months of
eating plums in a cuckoo clock—

she in her wicker rocker
brings sunlight into the room
plump fingers, aged, a force
frayed black of a cloth purse
single gold clasp, click
snap, a hand dives in and pennies
one by one emerge
in her gingerfingers for a grandson
her dress bright red, the sweater
wool, silver hair frilled
philosophic, abundant, curled
buckle black cork shoes
zinnias in her hair
silver worms on a dimestore chain
around her neck
the crease of her memory like heaven
flute colored lipgloss
slow copper, her grandson
he is seven and has fifteen,
sixteen, seventeen, eighteen
rich for the movies—

it is 1939 like the Hudson
and the last LaSalle
Uncle Triller's Cord was lark yellow

in her room with her music
father's stamp magnifying glass
to read the bible, *Collier's*
The Saturday Evening Post
icons like farmers
from the land of the ghosts
in the window the grandmother
the heritage, surveyor, sacrilegious
if she were not so kind
so despicable, so loved
hunched like an oilwitch, smiles—
even kings die
trying to make life whole
men in rowboats, whales, oars
playing in traffic the freeway
moves from prime time to prime time
flower blossoms in winter
no marshmallows for our chocolate
hot and spiced with brandy
cows and a horse, chickens
a pine tree in our livingroom
with Christmas lights
pretzels, Chinese dolls
a new electric train and village—

the attic is noisy with new mice
the grandmother says it's a good life
this farm is exorcised because
it is part of the earth
like the family that lives here and
the blackbirds
that nest on our roof.

Jon Stefan

BIG BULL CABLE

It takes a big man
to fold away like that
and spin past him in
a broken lake
telling us all about
the fun he never had.
It takes a big horse of a man
all right to reach down and cut
off his tail when it starts
to shake white circles around
blue moon lakes.
It takes a big man all right
to look at life and not run
the other way,
and Big Bull Cable was that man
pulling in all his chains
burning up in a one man lake.
Big Bull Cable headed out for
the country to gaze upon a year
that had gone to waste.

John Svehla

A BLOWN BIRD

Nebula of a hot afternoon
balloon
drying in the desert flats
close the wind
early sand
a blown bird.

                John Svehla

A RUSTY WIND

Leaves grow up into blooms
and fall down from the trees
in the cracking shadow
of the grass hills

gray mackerel houses
shrivel up and dry out
in the wind.

                John Svehla

AMNESIA

I was cooking. The
Child called, "The snow
outside is blue." I
Went, of course. In

The shadows he pointed:
Oaken shadows in that late
Afternoon were deep blue: sky

After a storm. He took my
Hand and led me away from
The house, knocking snow-domes
Off the top of fence-posts
As he walked.

David Swain

COOL AIR

Ghosts swept into my room at dawn.
They came through the screen,
Each hole making a tiny perforation
In their souls.
They touched me with cool brush strokes,
Caressed my skin with their embrace,
Speaking silently,
Saying nothing.

David Swain

EL MORRO

Great white ship through desert scrub surging,
Ancient profile of mighty power,
High-floating guarder of magic mystic spring—
Who came today, came yesterday, comes tomorrow,
I saw it first, as did he, and so will you.

Cryptic markings on the wall by self-historians—
Age-old shelter-place for desert-strider,
Leaving hieroglyphs to prove he lived,
Before vanishing forever along the valley,
Creating himself like you and me and him.
Names and dates and plaints scratched by dons,
By pedros, where cool-shaded haven
Escapes the noon, their bits of history
Record. And riders west their notes inscribed
To make this rock a point in human time.
Who could resist writing on white walls
That climb above the plain? But your marks
Or mine deface, they say, this monument in sunny space.
So I let them sleep, the self-sayers
And I spring from ledge to ledge
Rising up the mesa towards the sky.
Spreading out below flow distances
Of olive plain towards misty mountains—
Space is blue, green, brown, and far-off pink.
No wonder here built houses the human finders
Of the great white rock!

Across the top of the world I step.
Far away girls flutter, coming across the mesa,
Some in lilting skirts, some in faded jeans.
Twittering like swallows, they sing to each other
And to me. They flit across the mesa
In two and threes, stopping here and there,

Little maids in white, in blue, in lemon,
Laughing. "Hi," one calls. "Hi, hi," echoes come.
"Hi," I say, and smile, and see them smile.
One-by-one they lightly pass,
Nubile spirits of the great white sky-touching rock.

W. Edgar Vinacke

THE SILVER FOREST

When the mushroom clouds upward spring
From the monstrous craters left below
Where no thing lives nor can longer live
To spread across the world a layer of lethal dust
To rain down its poison for who knows how long—
I'll walk by day and night
Over hills and through valleys to find
Where I can stay immune and safe
Knowing not as no one will know
Whether morning will come or darkness
Forever fall.

When the sun, a raging purple bruise
Oozing through its spreading shroud
Failing falls to the edge of night,
I'll drop to sleep among the firs and ferns
Which will linger green until tomorrow,
For one must sleep though morning never comes.
I'll sleep as if sleep can send away
Any terror, as if health will come
When I awake and life will grow again
To breathe and throb.

While the molten moon grimaces through its mourning veils,
I'll hear choruses of voices,
Tenor, bass, soprano, alto, vibrant
Notes of love that rise and sink, and join and part—
Waking me, the song will wind among the trees,
Now gay, now a sighing strain,
As lovers speak.

I'll stand beneath the faintly burning moon,
Swaying, wondering, as when a child
I felt magic in the shadowed night,
What mystery urges me out there.
Through the forest I'll steal, afraid the song will end,
Where enchanting silver gleam the leaves
Where silver shimmers underfoot and twinkles
When a breeze creeps through the trees.
Silver dust will glisten, will sift down,
As if the singing will make the air
A silver dance.

Through the silver mists I'll see
Young women undulate and young men arch seductive steps,
Sadly nude with silver hair and silver skin,
Dancing at the end of time, when all is gone,
Save only they, who want the long embraces
Love gives in hopeful times. They chorus
Bravely, silver midnight children, kissing
When they meet, parting, glancing sidelong,
Languid, sensuous, ready for love,
Wanting love before too late the night will go.
Eyes downcast, smooth silver arms as graceful
As in the glide of silver stars, bodies twisting,
Drugged with love, breasts uplifted, the maidens dance,
Penises erect, the young men dance,
Singing, turning to each other, silvery,
Ready for love.

While the others sing, a young man will a maiden sweep
Into his arms and lightly run to vanish
At the silver forest's edge,
And those who remain will swell the song
And onward dance in heart-full ecstacy,
Waiting their turns to join and fly
Where the others go to love each other
While still they can.

Two-by-two they'll flit away, stirring silver dust,
Song adrift in space, calling
To a far-off world still green and full of life
Where lovers dance and wake to sing
Another day.

        W. Edgar Vinacke

AT THE PAIN OF DEATH

Over the generations
he amassed great wealth
from his grocery stores.

In his last years
he set out on his mission:
That his will would go on unimpeded.

His agents went about quietly,
rigging the one item
in all his stores
that had been his passion
and key to immortality;
Each parcel wired to a thermonuclear device.

I was at his side when he expired.
I am still shaken
by his insane laughter
and last words,
"Even in death,
Mr. Whipple alone squeezes Charmin!"

This is how civilization shall end.

I alone know.

                                        Michael E. Waldecki

SOCIALLY TYRANNOSAUR

Gathering
In the silence
Look upon our measure
Evoking the comfort
and wisdom of self-esteem.

Our stealth and hunger—
The wounded
Learning to discount
The blood that streams from our mouths
The sound of tearing flesh
The small cries

Our children run from us screaming
As we dwell
In the smoke of our laughter.

Michael E. Waldecki

THE ICE HOLDS TIGHT

to the doll's hair
not yielding her
to the child's tug.
She's been frozen
by the porch stairs
all winter now,
her open blue eyes
unblinking in snow,
and though it's March
the ice grips hard
to long yellow hair
not giving in
even to tears.

Cornered in this last
shady enclave the ice
gathers strength in the night,
battling back over
the no-man's land
between porch and garage
again and again
with the kindling spring sun,

asking no quarter,
giving none.

                              Marty Walsh

SIMON SAYS

my body's
an uncomfortable
house,
the rooms
institutional green,
crooked photographs
of plastic flowers
hang on the walls,
the plumbing
hasn't worked
since he's been staying
here,
the screen door
bangs
coming and going
but no one's ever there—
try to make yourself at home,
the doctor says,
but Simon
doesn't sleep under his bed
making up bad dreams,
Simon doesn't knot
his shoelaces
when he's not looking,
Simon doesn't grind
his teeth
too loud in his head,
Simon doesn't get hard
in his pants,
Simon doesn't say
gimme, gimme, gimme
and leer, tongue
working, at the nurses.

Today, Simon is suffocating
in a cramped, dark closet.
The doctor
is down on his knees
examining Simon through
the keyhole
with a pen flashlight;
we converse about his condition
indirectly, in undertones,
then the doctor writes
Simon a prescription,
slips it under the door,
and gets up and goes.

    . . .

Simon says
you may not go
to sleep tonight,
Simon says
a black cat
crossed your path
today,
Simon says
you may not
unzip your fly,
Simon says
throw salt
over your shoulder
for good luck,
Simon says...

                          Marty Walsh

GRETEL

No cameras allowed beyond this point.
As you can see the area behind me
has been cordoned with rope,
and is off limits to photos and journalists.
Certain facts have been established though:
it was here in the Black Forest
at this secluded woodcutter's cottage
that the incidents began about three weeks ago.

(The fog hadn't lifted when Gretel woke up.
The loft she lay in smelled of damp woodsmoke.
She could hear someone moving around downstairs.
Then the cock crowed. But something was wrong.
Then she remembered. The Old Witch, as she
and Hans called Step-Mother behind her back,
had finally won. Daddy was going to do what she
wanted. Hans hadn't heard them plotting
in the dark last night. Then Daddy promising,
and then later still thrashing sounds
and heavy breathing and stifled moans.
And later still Step-Mother's laugh.
Oh, what do I care, Gretel thought,
and turned her face to the wall. Let me die.
Her stomach ached. Still she didn't reach
for the bread crust she'd saved. Poor Hans,
I almost want to give it to him. He looks
so thin. But we'll need it for the plan
I thought up).

We have reports from reliable sources
that the two runaway children, who live here,
allegedly had something do to
with the spectacular fire we reported last night
at the historic Gingerbread House and Restaurant.

The Gingerbread House, which had been closed
down for the winter season, caught fire
around dinner time and burned to the ground.
The Polizei report hard evidence that at least three
squatters were unlawfully occupying the House
at the time that the incident took place.
The Coroner's Office has confirmed rumors
that the ash and bone of a human being—
believed to be that of a female part-time
employee, who, it is surmised, had a key
to the building—was found in the Gingerbread
Restaurant's main fireplace oven. The children,
whose names are being withheld because they
are minors, are said to be still missing.
The children's unemployed father has, thus far,
been cleared of all charges—
though he can't explain why both his children,
and now his second wife, are missing.
Foul play is, according to Chief Inspector Lentz,
still not ruled out.
This is Roger Topliff reporting
from the Schwarzwald—and now back to you
in New York, Lincoln.

(Daddy in jackboots—
what a man you are!
black epaulets, eye patch,
striding to your place
at the head of the kitchen table.
It's an open secret
you used to always win
our family quarrels
(how I adored you)
without ever having to
so much as rattle your sword.

You put guts in the Word
and personally scare me
half to death, sir.
But I remember how we'd take pails
and walk together to the edge of the wood—
we picked raspberries
and I fed you half my share
while you sat on your haunches
like my cuddly bear—and then She came along.
O Daddy—you with the stiff-armed salute
and the tender neck bites—
take your naked bayonet
and run it through my heart
and stomach again and again!
Why can't you still love me
like you love that old witch?

I swear, Daddy,
I'll get even with her
if it's the last thing
I ever do).

                                    Marty Walsh

THE JAPANESE PRINT

The serene man
seated under the cherry tree
in the Japanese print
has not lived in the 20th Century.

The hermit
with his brazier and solitude,
his garden patch and smooth face,

The holy one
towards whose hut
a burdened woodcutter humps
up the mountain path,
emerging just above gathering cloud mist,

The master,
he who is both the Lotus
and the void,

The simple man
whose grey charcoal smoke whitens
rising to heaven above Hiroshima,

has not lived in the 20th Century.

Marty Walsh

MOONBEAM

Moonbeam playing on my pillow,
Let me ride your gentle light.
Take me high above the willow.
Take me with you on your flight.
Let me meet your friends up high,
The sparkling stars up in the sky.
And on a cloud, I'll rest my head.
Sweet moonbeam, tuck me into bed.

                                  Joan Yarnell

SHADOWS OF GREY

You've painted your life with shadows of grey,
And you long for the colors you knew yesterday.
Your life, like a canvas that no one else sees,
Has been warped from endless, aching needs.
I yearn for the day when I look in your eyes,
And I won't see the hurt you try to disguise.
And we could begin our own canvas some day
That wouldn't be painted with shadows of grey.

                                  Joan Yarnell

GABRIEL

There is a bond with you and I
that few could understand.
We smell it in the summer winds,
And feel it in the land.

Our shadows mingle through the field
that gladly yields beneath your strength.
And frolic seems to have no end,
and distance seems to have no length.

We run with love and loyalty
to places in the sun,
and two hearts beating wild and free,
are, for an instant, only ONE.

                              Joan Yarnell

CONTRIBUTOR NOTES

David A. Adams (Bird Island, MN) has published in *New Infinity, Wormwood, Lowlands, riverSedge, River Styx, Interstate, Mill, Total Abandon, Salome, Jump River* and other publications.

James C. Baloian (Fresno, CA) has published three books of poetry: *Poems; Down at the Santa Fe Depot: 20 Fresno Poets;* and *Ararat Papers*. His poems have appeared in numerous magazines and periodicals.

Dr. Panos D. Bardis (Toledo, OH) is Editor-in-Chief and book review editor of the *International Social Science Review* and the *International Journal on World Peace*. He has published fifteen books, including a novel, *Ivan and Artemis,* and an anthology of poems, *Nine Oriental Muses*.

Steven Ronald Brattman (Los Angeles, CA) is a graduate of UCLA. He has been published in magazines of Great Britain, France, New Zealand, Rhodesia, Canada, as well as in the United States.

Marilyn Salzl Brinkman (Albany, MN) is "a central Minnesota writer and farm woman." She coauthored *Light From the Hearth,* a nonfiction book about central Minnesota pioneers and their architecture. She has published poetry in *Women's Times, Truly Fine Press, Wheatsprouts,* and in local publications.

Wendy C. Brooks (South Hadley, MA) has published in *Cambric Poetry Project Three, The Poet,* and *The Earthwise 1983 Calendar*.

Judith Cody (Los Angeles, CA) has published in *Sequoia, Stonecloud, Foreground, Androgyne,* and other literary magazines. Her poetry also appears in *The Miniature An-*

thology, Amphichoria, The Atlantic Monthly Press and *World's Best Loved Poems.* Judith composes classical guitar music for the concert stage.

Elaine Dallman (Reno, NV) is founder of Women-In-Literature, Inc. and editor-in-chief of *Woman Poet.* She has been active in programs that bring poets and poetry directly in to the community. Elaine has published over 170 poems in a broad variety of literary anthologies and journals.

Laura Dennison (Brooklyn, NY) has published poetry in both popular and literary magazines. She is a member of Poets & Writers, Inc.; Mensa; the French Institute; and the American Museum of Natural History. She has been a teacher, a secretary, and a member of the Democratic Party.

Gwen S. Fick (Lakeside, OH) has had poems and stories through the Firelands Writing Center (Huron, OH), in *The Dreamshop,* and *Cambric Poetry Project Three.* Gwen has been a winner in the annual Ohio Poetry Day contests for three consecutive years.

John Gery (New Orleans, LA) is the author of *Charlemagne: A Song of Gestures* (1983). He currently teaches at the Univ. of New Orleans.

Arthur Ginsberg (Seattle, WA) is a physician and has been writing poetry for ten years. He has appeared in *American Poetry Anthology, Embers,* and *Totem.* His manuscript, "Walking the Panther," won the 1983 Totem book publishing contest and is now in print.

Catherine Grogan (King of Prussia, PA) has publications in *Pinchpenny, Poetry North, Day Tonight/Night Today, Rebirth of Artemis, Mati,* and *The Yellow Butterfly.*

Richard F. Hay (Newton, MA) is a captain in the Newton Fire

Department. He writes: "Five of my poems, none of which were accepted by Cambric Press, were accepted in a booklet entitled "Late Harvest."

Mary Ann Henning (St. Louis, MO) has appeared in earlier Poetry Projects. Her first book of poetry, *The Conquering Hero,* has just been released by the Cambric Press.

Susan A. Katz (Monsey, NY) writes and teaches poetry. She has appeared in *The American Scholar, Kansas Quarterly, Prism International, The Anthology of Magazine Verse, Yearbook of American Poetry*, and other magazines. Susan has a chapbook, "The Separate Sides of Need" (1984) and a full-length collection, *Two Halves of the Same Silence,* to be published spring 1985.

Judy Klare (Athens, OH) has been writing poetry for over fifty years. She has published in college literary magazines and other periodicals.

Aaron Kramer (Oakdale, NY) has published *Seven Poets in Search of an Answer* (1944); *The Poetry of Heine* (1948); *Rumshinsky's Hat* (1964); *On the Way to Palermo* (1973); *Carousel Parkway* (1980); and *The Burning Bush* (1983). He co-edits *West Hills Review: a Whitman Journal.*

Jack Lindeman (Fleetwood, (PA) has published two books, *Twenty-One Poems* (1963) and *The Conflict of Convictions* (1968). His poems have appeared in *The Beloit Poetry Journal, Commonweal, The Massachusetts Review, The Nation, New World Writing, Poetry, Prairie Schooner, Southern Poetry Review, Southwest Review,* and others.

Mary Peat McDonald (Norwalk, OH) has published in *Cambric Poetry Project Three, The Voice, Poetry is Living in the Firelands; The Main Wale; The Plough,* and *International Cat Fancy Magazine.*

Raeburn Miller lives in New Orleans, LA.

Clare Mills (Bellevue, OH) is a railroad engineer who reads his poetry throughout northern Ohio. Among his credits are *Cambric Project Three* and *The Plough: North Coast Review.* He is a member of the Firelands Writing Center, the Poet's League of Greater Cleveland, and Writers' Resource Center of Toledo.

Susan Packie (Belleville, NJ) teaches anthropology at Malcolm-King College in Harlem and has had poetry, short stories, articles and reviews in numerous publications.

Thomas Paladino (Boston, MA) edits *The Third Wind,* a journal of poetry and myth. Recent poems have appeared in *West Hills Review, Zone* and *Telescope.* In 1983, the first two books of his sequential poem-in-progress, *Presences,* were published in one volume by Charles River Press.

Michael Joseph Phillips (Bloomington, IN) has published over 700 traditional and experimental poems. His book on the poet Edwin Muir was recently published as was a volume of poetry, *Superbeuts* (Cambric Press, 1983), which has gone into a second printing.

J.F. Pytko lives in Huntington Beach, CA.

Odiel Sainte lives in New York City.

Dr. M. P. A. Shaeffer (Millersville, PA) has appeared in little magazines throughout the U.S. and in anthologies published by the American Poetry Association and the Indiana Univ. of Pennsylvania Press. She has received awards from North American Mentor, the APA, and the Arizona Poetry Association.

Jon Stefan (Tucson, AZ) has written for *The New York Times; Poetry; People Magazine; the Christian Science Monitor;*

Aloha, the Magazine of Hawaii; National Review; and *Encore Magazine.* He has appeared in *Cambric Poetry Project Two* and *Three.*

John Svehla (Hollywood, CA) has publications which include *Sun* ("a small book"), *Pigiron Press, Spafaswap, Calif. Federation of Chaparral Poets, Pennsylvania Poetry Society, Look Quick, Wind Literary Journal, The Poet, Cambric Poetry Project Three, Earthwise Literary Calendar* and *Fine Arts Press.*

David Swain lives in Amherst, MA.

W. Edgar Vinacke (Buffalo, NY) is Professor Emeritus of Psychology at State Univ. of New York at Buffalo. He has appeared in previous *Cambric Poetry Projects.*

Michael E. Waldecki (Lorain, OH) has appeared in *Cambric Poetry Project Three, Colorado North Review, Nit & Wit, Bogg,* and *Pudding.* In addition to writing, his interests include theoretical physics, cosmology, and photography. His book, *The Electric, Vol. I,* was published in 1983.

Marty Walsh (Herman, ME) has published in *Beloit Poetry Journal, Willow Springs Magazine, Stone Country, Phoebe, Poem, Chinook, Hiram Poetry Review,* and previous *Cambric Poetry Projects.*

Joan Yarnell lives in Grove, OK.